YOUR KNOWLEDGE HAS VALUE

- We will publish your bachelor's and master's thesis, essays and papers

- Your own eBook and book - sold worldwide in all relevant shops

- Earn money with each sale

Upload your text at www.GRIN.com and publish for free

Bibliographic information published by the German National Library:

The German National Library lists this publication in the National Bibliography; detailed bibliographic data are available on the Internet at http://dnb.dnb.de .

This book is copyright material and must not be copied, reproduced, transferred, distributed, leased, licensed or publicly performed or used in any way except as specifically permitted in writing by the publishers, as allowed under the terms and conditions under which it was purchased or as strictly permitted by applicable copyright law. Any unauthorized distribution or use of this text may be a direct infringement of the author s and publisher s rights and those responsible may be liable in law accordingly.

Imprint:

Copyright © 2001 GRIN Verlag, Open Publishing GmbH
Print and binding: Books on Demand GmbH, Norderstedt Germany
ISBN: 9783656277286

This book at GRIN:

http://www.grin.com/en/e-book/797/the-first-transcontinental-railroad

Moritz Oehl

The First Transcontinental Railroad

GRIN Publishing

GRIN - Your knowledge has value

Since its foundation in 1998, GRIN has specialized in publishing academic texts by students, college teachers and other academics as e-book and printed book. The website www.grin.com is an ideal platform for presenting term papers, final papers, scientific essays, dissertations and specialist books.

Visit us on the internet:

http://www.grin.com/

http://www.facebook.com/grincom

http://www.twitter.com/grin_com

Otto-Friedrich-Universität Bamberg
Fakultät Sprach- und Literaturwissenschaften – Fach: Anglistik
Proseminar "The Geography, History, Folklore, and Literature of American Transportation"

Sommersemester 2001

The First Transcontinental Railroad

Moritz Oehl

Studiengang: MA Anglistik (NF: KoWi, BWL)
Semesterzahl: 03

Table of Contents

1. Introduction 3
2. Still a long way to go… 3
   2.1 The System of Transportation in the US before 1860 .. 3
   2.2 Importance of a Transcontinental Railroad 4
   2.3 The Preparations begin 5
3. Linking the Oceans 6
   3.1 Working Details and Methods 7
   3.2 The Welding of the States 8
   3.3 Consequences of the first Transcontinental Railroad. 9
4. Summary 10
Bibliography: 12

1. Introduction

The building of the first Transcontinental Railroad marks one of the highlights in American History. Nearly 20,000 workers, mostly immigrants or Chinese, especially engaged for this job, had build a line stretching from Omaha, Nebraska, to the eastern boundary of California within just six years. This largest project in the history of American transportation cost about $ 50 Mio., a number not reached ever before. Huge discussions preceded the project, even more were held afterwards. This termpaper will deal with the preparations for, the actual work and the consequences of this enormous construction.

2. Still a long way to go...

2.1 The System of Transportation in the US before 1860

Until 1825, when the Erie Canal was opened, the few existing land routes to the west were very dangerous. Only beyond the Mississippi River transportation on roads was suitable, for there the rivers were bad to travel on.

By 1860 the system of railroads in the U.S. was only well developed in the regions of the thirteen first colonies and in the Midwest. The only way into the North American interior was along the waterways. The railways which existed just reached as far as the Mississippi (South) and the Missouri (North, St. Joseph).[1]

---

[1] Cf. Handouts Bamberg SS 2001 (2001: 40)

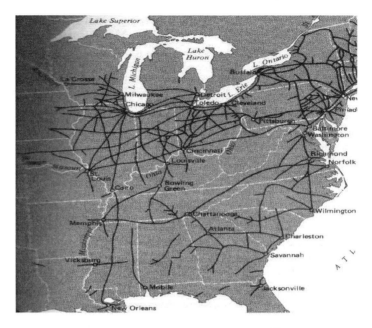

Fig. 1: US railway system by 1860[2]

2.2 Importance of a Transcontinental Railroad

As Americans realized that there were lands, natural resources and lots of possibilities in the West, first thoughts of constructing a railway to Oregon arose. The first person to start the public discussion of building such a Transcontinental Railroad was Asa Witney, a New York merchant, in 1845. He was convinced that without this railway the then independent region of Oregon would separate and become a sovereign state. Witney therefore addressed the following to the 28th Congress:

"[…] the time is not far distant when Oregon will become a State of such
magnitude and importance as to compel the establishment of a separate
Government – a separate nation, which will have cities, ports, and harbors,
all free, inviting all the nations of the earth to a free trade with them;
when they will control and monopolize the valuable fisheries of the Pacific;
control the coast trade of Mexico and South America, of the Sandwich Islands,
Japan, and all China, and be our most dangerous and successful rivals in the
commerce of the world. But your memorialist believes that this road will unite
them to us, enabling them to receive the protecting care of our Government,
sharing in its blessings, benefits, and prosperity, and imparting to us our

---

[2] Martin (1992: 47)

share of the great benefits from their local position, enterprise and industry."[3]

But Congress took no definite action. Time went on and public thought changed: Was Oregon the best solution regarding the western end of the railway?
On January 24, 1848, an event in California finally determined the path of the route: rich gold deposits, found on the American River, caused another "Goldrush". The news spread throughout the West and reached the middle and Atlantic states by late summer. "The acquirement of nearly a million square miles of additional territory toward the West and Southwest[4], coupled with the discovery of gold and the resultant overland rush by hundreds of thousands of people, made it apparent to the whole country that a pacific railway had become a pressing necessity".[5] The situation had changed: now people favoured the Bay of San Francisco as the logical western end of the railway.

2.3 The Preparations begin

The necessity of constructing a line through the mostly unexplored and uninhabited space between the area west of the Mississippi and the Sierra Nevada mountain range became more and more pressing. In 1853 Congress passed an act providing for a survey of several lines from the Mississippi to the Pacific[6]. It took nine more years until the operation finally started: with the creation of the "Union Pacific Railroad Company", together with the amending Act of 1864, a corporation was authorized to construct a railway from "an initial point on the one hundreth meridian of longitude"[7] to the eastern bay of California. On the other hand, the "Central Pacific Company of California" got permission to start building from Sacramento to the state line. The idea behind this separation was to let the two companies meet each other and form a junction.

---
[3] Dunbar (1915: 1327)
[4] By the treaty of peace with Mexico in 1848 the US had come into possession of a large region in the western part of the continent now occupied by the states of Arizona, California, Nevada, New Mexico, Texas, Utah, and parts of Colorado and Wyoming
[5] Dunbar (1915: 1333)
[6] Cf. Moody (1919: 122)
[7] Moody (1919: 123)

The "Central Pacific" was founded by Theodore Judah. He had found a way to lay tracks across the Sierra Nevada Mountains of California, one of the most complicated parts of the project. His counterpart on the side of the "Union Pacific" was Thomas C. Durant. [8] The Government also played an important part in the construction, viz. by financial support:

> "For the main line and the authorized branches[9], aid was to consist of ten sections per mile and a first mortgage loan[10] of $ 16,000 per mile for the eastern and western parts, of $ 48,000 per mile for 140-mile-stretches in the Rocky and Sierra Nevada Mountains respectively, and of $ 32,000 per mile in the Great Basin between them [...] their total for the mainline was not to exceed $ 50,000,000." [11]

Additionally to this enormous credit, the "Union Pacific" and the "Central Pacific" (plus other railroad companies not involved into this project) were given so-called "land grants"[12]: from 1862 to 1872, "Congress gave away more than 100 million acres of public land to railroad companies and provided them with over $ 64 million in loans and tax breaks". [13] The preparations were now done and work had to begin.

3. Linking the Oceans

The actual construction of the first Transcontinental Railroad began in 1864, shortly after the law of 1862 had been amended[14]. As has been already said, the "Union Pacific" started from Omaha, advancing westwards, and the "Central Pacific" began building at the same time, starting from Sacramento, California.

---

[8] Cf. http://www.pbs.org/wgbh/amex/iron/index.html
[9] The Railroad Companies additionally had to construct branches, leading away from the transcontinental route
[10] a legal agreement by which a bank or similar organization lends you money to buy a house, etc., and you pay the money back over a number of years
[11] Goodrich (1960: 183)
[12] Cf. Martin (1992 : 281)
[13] Levine et. Al (1989: 516-523)
[14] This was done by the act of July 2nd; the actual construction began only shortly afterwards

3.1 Working Details and Methods

A pamphlet form by the Union Pacific road in the summer of 1868 describes the different working groups involved in the construction in a detailed manner:

> "The graders go first. There are 2,000 of them. Their advance is near the Black Hills, and their work is done to Julesburg. Of the tie-getters and woodchoppers there are 1,500. Their axes are resounding in the Black Hills, over Laramie Plains, and in the passes of the Rocky Mountains. They have 1,000,000 ties in these hills awaiting safeguards [soldiers] for trains to haul them. Then follow the tie-layers, carefully performing their share of the work."[15]

In total, more than 20,000 men were involved in building the railroad. Most of them were immigrants: "The Central Pacific employed almost 10,000 Chinese workers; Union Pacific laborers ware mainly from Europe – Irishmen, Germans, Dutch, and Czechoslovakians. Thousands of Civil War veterans also worked on the Union Pacific".[16] As work could not only be done by men, so-called "Construction Trains" and "Boarding Cars" were needed:

> "Now go back twenty miles on the road, and look at the immense construction trains, loaded with ties and rails, and all things needed for the work [...] Six miles back are other trains of like character. These are the second line. Next, near the terminus, and following it hour by hour, are the boarding cars and a construction train, which answer to the actual battle line [...] The boarding cars go in advance. They are pushed to the extremity of the track; a construction train then runs up, unloads its material and starts back to bring another from the second line ... The trucks, each drawn by two horses, play between the track-layers and their supplies. One of these trucks takes on a load of rails, about forty, with the proper proportion of spikes and chairs, making a load, when the horses are started off on a full gallop for the track-layers. On each side of these trucks are rollers to facilitate running off the iron."[17]

After this was done, the rest was up to laborers again:

> "The rails within reach, parties of five men stand on either side. One in the rear throws a rail upon the rollers, three in advance seize it and run out with it to the proper distance. The chairs have, meantime, been set under the last rails placed. The two men in the rear, with a single swing, force the end of the rail into the chair, and the chief of the squad calls out 'Down', in a tone that equals the 'Forward' to an army. Every thirty seconds there came that brave 'Down,' 'Down', on either side the track."[18]

After only a small part of the line had been build, the companies longed for more financial support. As a result, the

---

[15] Dunbar (1915: 1352)
[16] http://www.pbs.org/wgbh/amex/iron/index.html
[17] Dunbar (1915: 1352-1353)
[18] Dunbar (1915: 1353)

"Credit Mobilier of America" was founded – a subletting company which from now on managed the construction and its financial part. Its name was derived from the "famous investment banking firm that had marshalled immense amounts of capital to build the French railroad system in the 1850s".[19] Only two years later (1866) this decision seemed to work: over five hundred miles of the line had been build.[20] Besides, the "Credit Mobilier" had another function: if the project worked well, stockholders of the company would receive handsome dividends – the profits of the construction.[21]

3.2 The Welding of the States

In the early spring of 1869 the prospect that the road would be finished soon grew more and more apparent. While in the beginning construction had been very slowly, the two companies had gained more and more rapidity in the last few months and were, in spring 1869, only divided by "a gap of about one hundred feet".[22] Of the last few steps in this monumental construction of the 1860's is told as follows:

> "On 10 May 1869 from Promontory Summit northwest of Odgen, Utah, a single telegraphed word, 'done', signaled to the nation the completion of the first Transcontinental Railroad [...] Union Pacific's No. 119 and Central Pacifics 'Jupiter' engines lined up facing each other on the tracks, separated only by the width of one rail [...] At 12:47 P.M. the actual last spike – an ordinary iron spike – was driven into a regular tie".[23]

---

[19] Martin (1992: 285)
[20] Cf. Moody (1919: 125)
[21] Cf. Martin (1992: 286)
[22] Dunbar (1915: 1354)
[23] http://www.media.utah.edu/UHE/g/GOLDENSPIKE.html

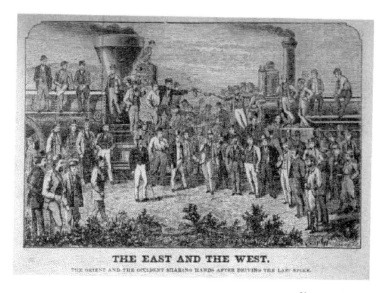

Fig. 2: Promontory Point, Utah, May 1869[24]

A work of national character was finished - now travelling 1775 miles from Omaha to Sacramento without changing the means of transportation was possible- something no one had dreamed of only few decades before.

3.3 Consequences of the first Transcontinental Railroad

As a result of the first Transcontinental Railroad, people began moving to the West. Moody describes the new situation as follows: "The vast El Dorado of the West was laid practically at the doorstep of Eastern capital. Not only did American pioneers turn definitely toward the West, but foreign emigrants bent their steps in vast numbers in that direction, and capital in steadily increasing amounts made its way there".[25] So in the 1860's and 70's many centers sprang up: Kansas City, Denver,

---

[24] Dunbar (1915: 1339)
[25] Moody (1919: 130)

Salt Lake City, Portland, Seattle, Minneapolis and many others developed due to the spread of the railroad.[26]
In total, railroad companies constructed 35,000 miles of railroad track in the USA from 1867-1873.[27] In these six years more roads were built than in the thirty years before the Civil War. Additionally more land was put under cultivation than ever before.

4. Summary

Initiated by a clever New York merchant (Asa Witney), lots of times discussed about by Congress, built within just six years - that was the first Transcontinental Railroad. A project unifying the East and the West, accompanied by the greatest land grants in US history ever and worth more than $ 50,000,000. The rapidity with which it was build was due to economic interests - the faster the road was completed, the earlier the two companies could earn money with it.
The first Transcontinental Railroad was a work of enormous efforts, which involved about 20,000 workmen constructing 1775 miles of railway track - from Omaha, Nebraska, through the Black Hills, leaving the Great Salt Lake behind, jumping over the Rocky Mountains and finally reaching the Bay of San Francisco with a view to the Pacific Ocean.
The consequences of this work are well known: people started moving to the West in greater abundance, settling alongside the railway track, and leaving no doubt that there would be any space in the States left which was not settled by Americans.
Today there is not much left: the two locomotives which had in 1869 joined at Promontory Point were both by 1903 scrapped for iron. Now only a park remains: "In 1957 Congress established a seven-acre tract as the Golden Spike National Historic Site" - including "walking and driving tours along the old grades, as well as to photo and other exhibits celebrating the transcontinental railroad".[28] Though the line has disappeared

---

[26] Cf. Moody (1919: 131)
[27] Levine et. Al. (1989 : 516-523)
[28] http://www.media.utah.edu/UHE/g/GOLDENSPIKE.html

nearly completely, the consequences of this enormous work will never be forgotten – the first Transcontinental Railroad was the "Settler of the West".

Bibliography:

- Dunbar, Seymour (1915): A History of Travel in America. Volume IV. Indianapolis. The Bobbs-Merrill Company.
- Goodrich, Carter (1960): Government promotion of American canals and railroads. 1800-1890. New York. Columbia University Press.
- Handouts Bamberg SS 2001
- Levine, Bruce / Brier, Stephen / Brundage, David / Countryman, Edward / Fennell, Dorothy / Rediker, Markus / Brown, Joshua (Eds.) (1989): Who Built America. Working People and the Nation's Economy, Politics, Culture, and Society (American Social History Project, City University of New York). Volume One: From Conquest and Colonization through Reconstruction and the Great Uprising of 1877. New York. Pantheon Books.
- Martin, Albro (1992): Railroads Triumphant. The Growth, Rejection, and Rebirth of a Vital American Force. New York / Oxford. Oxford University Press.
- Moody, John (1919): The Railroad Builders. A Chronicle of the Welding of the States. In: Johnson, Allen (Ed.): Abraham Lincoln Edition. Vol. 38. The Chronicles of America Series. Yale University Press. Newhaven.
- Blake, Deborah in: http://www.media.utah.edu/UHE/g/GOLDENSPIKE.html <20.11.01>
- http://www.pbs.org/wgbh/amex/iron/index.html <20.11.01>

YOUR KNOWLEDGE HAS VALUE

- We will publish your bachelor's and master's thesis, essays and papers

- Your own eBook and book - sold worldwide in all relevant shops

- Earn money with each sale

Upload your text at www.GRIN.com
and publish for free